IITT JUNIOR

5·6
LEVEL

International Interpretation &
Translation Test for Juniors

IITT JUNIOR: LEVEL 5-6

© 사단법인 국제통번역자원봉사단, 2019

1판 1쇄 인쇄 __ 2019년 04월 01일
1판 1쇄 발행 __ 2019년 04월 05일

지은이 __ 사단법인 국제통번역자원봉사단
펴낸이 __ 홍정표

펴낸곳 __ 글로벌콘텐츠
　　　　등록 __ 제 25100-2008-000024호

공급처 __ (주)글로벌콘텐츠출판그룹
　　　　대표 __ 홍정표 디자인 __ 김미미 기획·마케팅 __ 노경민 이조은 이종훈
　　　　주소 __ 서울특별시 강동구 풍성로 87-6(성내동) 1, 2층 전화 __ 02-488-3280 팩스 __ 02-488-3281
　　　　홈페이지 __ www.gcbook.co.kr

값 13,000원
ISBN 979-11-5852-236-0 13740

Learning English and practicing English are quite different in Korea. We have learned English as a school subject. But English is used as an important skills in the global society. We have a lot of chances to meet many English speaking people here and there. If we are not so good at communication skills in English, we face some difficulties. We have to find the best possible way to develop our communication skills.

In order to achieve this goal, students and teachers should do something different from book-based education. Students need to practice English as a language - not just for school tests in Korea. The need to read a lot of sentences aloud and practice saying them in conversational not only with their friends but also with naive English speakers.

In this course, students can find several different kinds of reading materials and essays. I do hope the students will not stop at reading and understanding this book, but also try to practice all materials with their friends and teachers. Try to play with the sentences without worrying about mistakes or faults. Just try to read the sentences as many times as possible untill you can read them very fast and fluently.

At last, you will find that you are able to read the sentences without watching every single word and understand the sentences without translating into Korean. Then you are ready to communicate in English. That is the real purpose of studying English and it can keep you become an English speaking person. Try to keep this practice untill you can use English as a communication tool.

In the first part, you may encounter very simple expressions with some familiar materials. I hope you can be accustomed to reading the materials aloud and repeating them several times until you can read and understand the materials without thinking about every word. Then you can make your own short sentences for yourself someday.

In the second part, you may find some more advanced reading materials and basic essays. They will develop you into better English speakers and writers. Using English in your daily life is very helpful to you. Most importantly, try your best to keep going with this book to the last page and you will know how to use basic English in common life.

Teachers can help their students to develop English and prepare for the IITT, International Interpretation & Translation Test. Students will take the test for interpretation and translation soon. They need to practice for dictation, listening, and translation into Korean or English composition. Finally, they will wite an English essay. They have to score over 80% to pass.

Good luck !

Table of Contents

IITT JUNIOR

International Interpretation & Translation Test for Juniors

Unit 01

New People

We call the first year students of a university, "Freshmen." Freshmen are newcomers to the school. They don't know many things about the school yet. They might feel lonely because they are beginning an unfamiliar lifestyle.

Therefore, teachers try to help them settle their campus lives. They will meet many new people like classmates, teachers, and even school administrators. All newcomers would like to meet more people in order to become accustomed to their new environment. Sooner or later, their confusion will settle down while adjusting themselves to their new circumstances.

So, what are the possible ways to adjust to the new environment? First, students can participate in programs for Freshmen such as the first year orientation. Next, students can join school clubs for interests such as music, sports, or movies. Finally, new students can meet their classmates and build strong relationships by talking about their dreams and sharing their special talents.

---

vocabulary

- environment: 환경
- participate: 참여하다(take part, join)
- relationship: 관계

1. Who are called 'Freshmen'?

2. Who can help the Freshman in campus?

3. What do the new students do to adjust the new environment?

Try to make a short sentence with the word or expression.

1. unfamiliar

2. be accustomed to

3. participate in

In our society, people have to work hard in order to make money. Also, companies want to hire new workers. In addition, job seekers, mostly in their twenties, are trying to get a job by improving their abilities.

Almost all companies hire new workers every year. In the case of a book company trying to hire a suitable employee, the company needs to find someone with the appropriate educational background. A person applying at a book company should also have special skills for publishing books such as proofreading or editing. When companies employ new workers, they try to develop their abilities and talents. In order for the new workers to adjust to their workplaces, they need to have specific skills that relate to their jobs.

Some might need computer skills and others need different talents. For example, fluency in foreign languages or having industry-specific knowledge of their field can help someone gain employment. In general, a lot of experiences will make a new employee a professional in the end.

vocabulary

- company: 회사, 동료
- job seeker: 구직자
- appropriate: 적절한(=fitting, suitable, relevant)

1. Why do people want to improve themselves?

   _____

2. What will you need to get a job at a book company?

   _____

3. What do you want to do to get a job in the future?

   _____

Try to make a short sentence with the word or expression.

1. in order to

   _____

2. apply to

   _____

3. in the end

   _____

(Nick and Helen meet at a party in L.A.)

Nick: Hi, are you from around here?

Helen: Oh! Hello there. No, I'm not. I am just visiting.

Nick: Let me introduce myself. I am Nick Jones, from Texas.

Helen: Nice to meet you, Nick. My name is Helen Parker. Call me Helen. I am from Ontario, Canada.

Nick: How long have you been here in L.A.?

Helen: I've been here for two days. How about you?

Nick: I have been here for a week now. How are you liking L.A. so far?

Helen: I like it very much. The weather is so nice and there are a lot of places to visit.

Nick: Have you toured around the city yet?

Helen: I was planning to do just that tomorrow. My friends are inviting me to eat at famous restaurants and to visit some of the landmarks here. I'm also hoping to at least see the Hollywood sign.

Nick: I hope you will enjoy yourself here and do the things that you like.

Helen: Thank you very much. Hope to see you again.

1. Where is Nick from?

   _____

2. How long has Helen been in L.A.?

   _____

3. Does Helen like L.A.?

   _____

Substitution Drills

1. Hi, are you from around here?
   - Hi, are you from this area?
   - Hi, are you from this town/city?
   - Hi, is this your hometown?

2. How are you liking L.A. so far?
   - Are you enjoying your stay in L.A. so far?
   - Are you having a good time here so far?
   - What do you think about L.A. so far?

3. Hope to see you again. (As a parting salutation)
   - See you soon.
   - Let's meet up soon.
   - Hope to see you around.

Fill in each blank with little, few, much, or many.

1. There is only a _____ water left in the jug. Leave some for me!

2. There are _____ toys all over the floor. Please put them away.

3. You put too _____ sugar in my coffee. It is too sweet now.

4. There is only a _____ rice in the pot. Please finish it.

5. _____ people came to the party because it was raining heavily.

6. Tom ate too _____ cakes. Now he has a stomachache.

7. Don't add too _____ salt to the soup. It is salty enough.

8. A _____ apples are left in the basket.

9. Mr Phua is carrying _____ bags. I wonder what is inside all of them.

10. There is not _____ food left after the party.

11. We have a _____ days to rehearse before the concert.

12. Please add a _____ lemon juice to the honey.

Unit 02

Career Satisfaction

Finding a Suitable Job

Nearly 50% of all workers have jobs they are not happy with. Don't let this happen to you. If you want to find a suitable job for you, don't rush through the ads in the newspaper. And, try to find such a job you will be happy with through the work.

According to psychologist John Holland, there are six types of personalities. For each type, there are certain jobs that might be right and others are probably wrong. Check your own type according to the following types.

The Realistic type is practical and likes working with machines or tools. The Investigative type is curious and likes to analyze situations. The Artistic type is imaginative and likes to express himself by creating art. The Social type is friendly and likes helping others. The Entertaining type is outgoing and active, so this type likes to persuade or lead other people. The Conventional type is careful and likes to follow routines.

If you can think about who you are, you can make the right job decision.

vocabulary

- pratical: 실용적인(=feasible)
- investigaive: 조사(수사)의
- persuade: 설득하다 (=talk(someone) into)

1. What kind of job will make you happy?

   _____

2. What is the Realistic type?

   _____

3. Why do we need to think about our personality?

   _____

Try to make a short sentence with the word or expression.

1. rush through

   _____

2. according to

   _____

3. persuade someone to

   _____

Strategies in Keeping your Job

You need to make sure that everyone knows you. Being a good worker is sometimes less important than making sure people know you are a good worker.

To keep your job, you need to learn everything that could make you do your job better. If the company buys new computers, learn how to use them even though you are not that familiar with them. In addition, be positive and active with whatever you have to do or are responsible for. It is also important to make sure you know everything about the company.

Also, improve your writing and speaking skills since it is necessary to keep your job. Having good ideas helps, but it isn't enough. You need to be able to communicate your ideas at any time. In the end, it all comes down to one basic strategy. Make yourself so valuable that the company won't want to lose you.

---

vocabulary

- positive: 긍정적인, 유익한(=beneficial, useful)
- responsible: (~을)책임지고 있는, 맡고 있는(=in charge)
- valuable: 소중한(=precious), 가치가 큰

1. Who is a good worker?

   _____

2. How can you make yourself valuable?

   _____

3. What can you do for your new position at a workplace?

   _____

Try to make a short sentence with the word or expression.

1. familiar with

   _____

2. learn how to

   _____

3. make yourself

   _____

SEE YOU LATER!

(Nick and Helen meet again at school)

Helen: Hello, Nick. How are you today?

Nick: Hi, Helen! I am very good, thanks. How about you?

Helen: I am fine, too. What are you going to do during this summer vacation?

Nick: I am planning to visit my grandparents.

Helen: Where do they live?

Nick: They live in Korea. They immigrated there when my grandfather retired from his job.

Helen: Wow, I heard it is a very beautiful country.

Nick: Yes, it is. I went there two years ago. I like Korea very much.

Helen: How long are you going to stay in Korea?

Nick: I will be there for three weeks.

Helen: That is quite a long time. What are you going to do first when you get there?

Nick: I am going to eat my favorite Korean foods, tteokbokki and kimchi fried rice.

Helen: I have eaten tteokbokki in Korea Town downtown.

Nick: Ah! But, experiencing it in Korea is way better.

Helen: I think so too. I hope to go to Korea someday. Have a good trip then.

Nick: Thanks a lot. See you later!

1. Where is Nick going to go during this summer?

   _____

2. Where do Nick's grandparents live?

   _____

3. How long is he going to stay in Korea?

   _____

1. How are you today?
   - How have you been doing?
   - What have you been up to?
   - How's life?

2. I am fine, too.
   - I am doing well, too.
   - I've never been better. (Never better.)
   - I feel wonderful / terrific / other adjectives.

3. Have a good trip then.
   - Enjoy your trip and stay safe.
   - Have a safe trip.
   - Bon Voyage! (French)

Fill in each blank with the plural form of the noun in the brackets.

1. The dog has just given birth to many _____ (puppy).

2. Posters of Santa Claus and his _____ (reindeer) are put up in department stores near Christmas time.

3. I broke my _____ (spectacles), so I must go to the optician.

4. Don't play with _____ (match). You may start a fire.

5. John loves strawberry milk but does not like to eat _____ (strawberry).

6. These two school _____ (bus) will take the children to the zoo.

7. Joel wanted to go to the airport to see the _____ (airplane) land and take off.

8. My father bought more _____ (fish) for his aquarium.

9. In autumn, the _____ (leaf) dried up and fell from the trees.

10. Mother is cooking curry tonight, so we need to buy a few _____ (loaf) of bread.

11. Cheyenne likes the _____ (story) because they're about _____ (fairy).

Jobs

If you want to visit another country or travel a long distance, the best type of transportation is usually an airplane. People take flights all over the world. Airlines are companies that provide flights for the public. Accordingly, the person who operates the plane and is the captain of the flight is called an airline pilot.

Airplanes are mostly very large and can carry hundreds of people. They fly thousands of feet high and usually fly for several hours in the sky. As a result, each plane usually has at least two pilots. The lead pilot is called the captain and the other pilot is called the co-pilot.

Flying a plane with so many passengers is an enormous responsibility. Airline pilots are responsible for the safety of every person on board. It is their job to make sure that every flight lands and takes off without any accidents. Even a small mistake can result in complete disaster. Therefore, airline pilots must be very focused and must be dependable people. Being a pilot is an important position for all passengers and all related people.

---

vocabulary

- transportation: 수송(운송), 교통수단
- operate: 작동되다, 가동하다(=run)
- disaster: 참사, 재난, 재해(=catasstrophe)

1. Who is a pilot?

2. Who is called a co-pilot?

3. What responsibilities does a pilot have?

Try to make a short sentence with the word or expression.

1. hundreds of

2. be responsibility of

3. on board

Most people have good friends and relatives. They usually live close to each other. They can meet and talk with them. In this situation, people don't have to send letters because they see each other in person.

In some cases, friends and relatives are living far away from one another. They cannot see each other very often. They want to hear from each other. They are eager to send their love and news to their friends and relatives.

Sending a letter is a good way to express their love. The person who carries the letter is called a postman. The postman helps people share their news. Of course, the news can be good or bad. However, there is a popular saying that comes to mind; "Don't blame the messenger."The contents of the news don't come from the postman.

<u>vocabulary</u>

• relatives: 친척(=kinsfolk)
• be eager to: 열망(갈망)하다(=be anxious to)

1. Who is a postman?

2. Why do we want to write a letter?

3. How can you express your love to your friends?

Try to make a short sentence with the word or expression.

1. relatives

2. far away

3. messenger

At the Airport

(James is standing in front of the ticket counter with his luggage)

Clerk: Good evening. Can I help you?

James: I want to check-in.

Clerk: Where are you going?

James: I am going to Vancouver, Canada.

Clerk: Okay. Your flight is Canadian Air flight 314 at 8:30 p.m. Can I see your passport and boarding pass?

James: Yes, here you are.

Clerk: Do you want a window seat or an aisle seat?

James: Window seat, please.

Clerk: Okay, you want a window seat. And how many bags do you have?

James: I have one.

Clerk: Okay. Here are your passport and boarding pass. Please proceed to gate 18.

James: Thank you very much.

Clerk: You're welcome. Have a nice trip.

1. Where is James going?

   _____

2. What time is James's flight?

   _____

3. How many bags does James have?

   _____

Substitution Drills

1. Can I help you?
   - How may I help you?
   - What can I do for you?
   - What can I help you with?

2. Yes, here you are.
   - Yes, of course. Here.
   - Yes, here they are.
   - Yes, here you go.

3. You're welcome.
   - My pleasure.
   - The pleasure is mine.
   - No problem. It was nice serving you.

Read each question carefully. Then, add an apostrophe ['] where necessary.

1. You should not open Fathers letter.

2. My grandfathers teapot is broken.

3. Which of these are the girls books? They are looking for their books.

4. That boys hamsters have escaped again!

5. The boys broke their mothers vase.

6. These are the pupils worksheets. They must complete the worksheets today.

7. This dogs nails need to be cut.

8. My neighbors fence is being repaired.

9. Why are you giving away Charles books?

10. James cat ate our parrot!

12. Mrs. Tangs dog tore the newspaper.

13. The womens cakes are very delicious.

Unit 04

Social Life

A social networking service is an online application or website that focuses on the building of social networks or social relations among people. For example, people share interests, backgrounds, thoughts, or make real-life connections online.

A social network service consists of a representation of each user, his/her social links, and a variety of additional information. Most social networking services are web-based and provide means for users to interact over the internet such as Twitter, Instagram, or Facebook.

Social networking services allow users to share ideas, activities, photos, and interests within their individual networks at any time. There have been attempts to standardize these services to avoid the need to duplicate entries on every platform.

A recent survey said that most adults and young people use at least one social networking service.

---

vocabulary

- connection: 관련성(=link), 교섭
- representation: 묘사, 표현
- interact: 소통하다, 교류하다, 교감하다

1. How can we build up a social relationship online?

2. What do we do in SNS?

3. What can we do within our individual networks?

Try to make a short sentence with the word or expression.

1. focus on

2. a variety of

3. standardize

Lesson 2　Making Plans with a Friend

Going out with a friend can be a great way to have fun and become closer. If you are thinking about asking a friend to do something, you should take some time and make a good plan. Your friend will appreciate your care and attention.

Firstly, you should choose a good time to meet your friend. You should consider your friend's schedule. You should know what day and time your friend is free. This way, your friend won't feel rushed or tired. It is important that your friend doesn't feel stressed during your time together.

Then, you can decide on a good place to go and what to do there. Try to think of food they like to eat or activities they like to do. Something new and exciting can also be a good idea. On the other hand, finding a quiet and peaceful place to have a good conversation can also help you build a stronger relationship.

---

vocabulary

- appreciate: 감사하다(=thank), 인정하다, 알아주다(=recongnize)
- peaceful: 평화로운, 비폭력적인

1. What can you do with your friends?

2. What do we need to consider to make a plan for a trip?

3. Why do we need to keep a friendship?

Try to make a short sentence with the word or expression.

1. appreciate

2. It is important to

3. On the other hand

At a Duty Free

(At a Duty Free shop, James is looking for presents for his family and friends back home in Canada)

Clerk: Good evening. May I help you find something?

James: I am looking for nice presents for my family and friends.

Clerk: What kind of present do you want?

James: I want to get traditional stuff.

Clerk: Okay. Let me suggest this gift set for your family. And, this stationery set for your friends.

James: What are in the sets?

Clerk: There are some traditional dolls and Korean cookies in the gift set. The stationery set contains a bookmark, pen, and Korean made paper. You may want to add more like key chains or some fans.

James: Hmm… I will buy two gift sets and three stationery sets. Also, give me two key chains and two fans please.

Clerk: Okay. Can I see your passport and boarding pass?

James: Here you are. How much is it?

Clerk: The total is 80 US dollars.

James: Here you go. Thank you.

1. What is James looking for at the Duty Free shop?

2. What did the clerk suggest James to buy?

3. How much is James going to pay for the present?

1. What kind of present do you want?
   - What presents are you looking for?
   - Are you looking for any particular things?
   - Do you have something in mind?

2. I want to suggest this gift set for your family.
   - I want to recommend this gift set for your family.
   - I suggest this gift set for your family.
   - Buying this gift set for your family is a good idea.

3. How much is it?
   - How much do I pay?
   - Please give me the total amount I need to pay.
   - How much does it cost?

The Indefinite Articles

Fill each blank with a or an to complete the sentences.

1. _____ apple a day keeps the doctor away.

2. Please lend me _____ pencil.

3. This is _____ waterproof watch.

4. It is raining. I need to borrow _____ umbrella.

5. Father is buying _____ new computer for me.

6. I saw _____ elephant at the zoo.

7. Each class will put up _____ item for the school concert.

8. This is _____ exciting book. I can't put it down.

9. That is _____ beautiful song.

10. She will peel _____ orange for us.

11. I ate _____ egg sandwich and drank _____ glass of milk for breakfast.

12. This is _____ picture of _____ unicorn.

13. It looks like _____ horse with _____ horn on its head.

Unit 05

Major Studies

The history of the world is the story of human beings. It started from the first civilization and continued to the space age. The story covers a period of about 5,000 years.

The early civilizations made many contributions to later generations. Probably the most important of these contributions was the invention of a system of writing, sometime before 3000 B.C. At that time, man started to write down a record of his life, and the period called Ancient Times or Ancient History began. And the period after writing began is called Historic Times.

Historians usually divide the whole span of Historic Times into four periods. They are Ancient Times, the Middle Ages, the Early Modern Era, and the Modern Era.

We study the history of the world to know ourselves.

---

vocabulary

- civilization: 문명
- contribution: 기여, 기부(=donation), 공헌

1. What is history?

2. What is the difference between Pre-historic and Historic Times?

3. Why do we study history?

Try to make a short sentence with the word or expression.

1. start from

2. make a contribution

3. divide the whole into

Literature, in its broadest sense, is everything that has ever been written. It includes comic books and pamphlets on potato bugs, as well as the novels of Mark Twain and the plays of William Shakespeare.

In a narrower sense, there are various kinds of literature. For example, we may read literature written in a certain language, such as French literature and Korean literature. We also study writings about a people such as the Native Americans. We often speak of the literature of a period, such as the literature of the 1800s. We also refer to the literature of a subject, as in the literature of gardening.

But, the word literature, in its strictest sense, means more than printed words. Literature is one of the fine arts. It refers to belles-letters, a French phrase that means beautiful writings. We distinguish between literature and comic books much as we distinguish between a professional baseball game and a backyard game of catch. When we speak of a piece of writing as literature, we are praising it.

---

vocabulary

- strict: 엄격한(=rigid)
- distinguish: 구별하다(=discriminate)

1. What is the literature in the widest sense?

   _____

2. What book genre do you like to read?

   _____

3. Tell me the name of a book you have read lately.

   _____

Language Acquisition

Try to make a short sentence with the word or expression.

1. potato bugs

   _____

2. distinguish between

   _____

3. refer to

   _____

This Vacation

(Minsu and Linda are eating dinner at a restaurant)

Minsu: How are you doing thesedays?

Linda: I'm good.

Minsu: I don't know what to do during this vacation. What's new with you?

Linda: I began reading a book last Monday. So, I'm learning new things.

Minsu: That's good. Did you buy the book?

Linda: No, I got it as a New Years present from my friend. It is actually Anne Frank's Diary.

Minsu: That's a very famous book. It is about a Jewish girl's life during the Nazi era, right?

Linda: That's right.

Minsu: Are you enjoying it?

Linda: So far, yes. But, according to the reviews, I might start tearing up soon because of the terrible things that she experienced.

Minsu: I heard about that too.

Linda: So, I am getting ready for the emotional roller coaster ride I am about to experience. Haha.

Minsu: Well, if it affects you that much, it means it is a good book, right?

Linda: I believe so.

Minsu: I might start reading a book too because of you.

Linda: That would be amazing!

Minsu: Well, I am not a book person but we'll see.

1. What has Linda been doing since last week?

   _____

2. Is Minsu busy nowadays?

   _____

3. Give a summary of what they are talking about.

   _____

1. That's right.
   - Correct.
   - Yes, you are correct.
   - Exactly.

2. I might start tearing up soon.
   - I might start crying soon.
   - I might be sad.
   - I might become emotional soon.

3. Emotional roller coaster ride…
   - Different emotions I will feel…
   - Feelings of happiness and sadness I will experience…
   - Both positive and negative feelings I will experience…

Rewrite each sentence by replacing the word or words in bold with a suitable personal pronoun.

1. Miss Lim is going to be our new teacher.

   _____

2. Isabelle and Claudia are best friends in school.

   _____

3. Where is Philip going to take his lunch?

   _____

4. Joel and I love to watch Sesame Street.

   _____

5. Are you going to visit your grandmother today?

   _____

6. Will you take Peter and Boon to the Night Safari?

   _____

7. I will return the books Mr. Ted tomorrow.

   _____

8. Please give Marlon and me the marbles now.

   _____

9. The dog is barking at the strangers.

   _____

10. Please do not frighten the cat.

   _____

Unit 06

Historic Sites

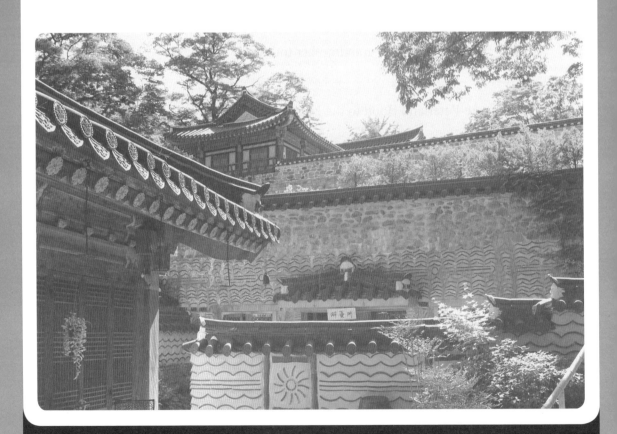

Gyeongbokgung, also known as Gyeongbok Palace, was the main royal palace of the Joseon dynasty. Built in 1395, it is located in northern Seoul, South Korea. It is the largest of the five Grand Palaces built by the Joseon dynasty.

Gyeongbokgung was the main palace of the Joseon dynasty until it was destroyed by fire during the Imjin War and abandoned for two centuries. However, in the 19th century, all of the palace's 7,700 rooms were restored. The architecture of ancient Korea was represented in this grand palace.

In the early 20th century, much of the palace was again destroyed by Japan. Since then, the palace has been reconstructed to its original form. Today, the palace is regarded as being the most beautiful of all the five palaces and many tourists visit it to appreciate this amazing historical site.

vocabulary

• dynasty: 왕조, (동일 가문에 속하는) 역대 통치자
• abandon: 포기하다(=give up)
• reconstruct: 재건(복원)하다

1. Which building is the largest among five Joseon palaces?

   _____

2. Why was Gyeongbok palace rebuilt?

   _____

3. Have you visited Gyeongbok palace? What did you see?

   _____

Try to make a short sentence with the word or expression.

1. be located in

   _____

2. abandon

   _____

3. regard as

   _____

The Great Pyramid of Giza is the oldest and largest of the three pyramids in the Giza pyramid complex in Egypt. It is the oldest of the Seven Wonders of the Ancient World. It was built in honor of the Pharaoh Khufu.

Archaeologists believe that the pyramid was built as a tomb at around 2560 BC. At 146.5 meters (481 feet), the Great Pyramid was the tallest man-made structure in the world for more than 3,800 years. Most people agree that it was built by thousands of workers moving huge stones and lifting them into place.

There are three chambers inside the Great Pyramid. The lowest chamber is below the pyramid and it is unfinished. The Queen's Chamber and King's Chamber are higher up within the pyramid structure. The main part of the Giza complex is made up of other buildings including smaller pyramids.

vocabulary

- complex: 복합건물, 단지
- chamber: 회의실, ~실

1. Where is the Giza Pyramid?

   _____

2. Who built the Giza Pyramid?

   _____

3. What can you see inside the Giza Pyramid?

   _____

Try to make a short sentence with the word or expression.

1. in honor of

   _____

2. man-made

   _____

3. be made up of

   _____

Language Practice: Q&A Activity

Try to answer the following brainteasers with your partner.

1. How many letters are there in "alphabet"?

2. How many months have 28 days?

3. A red house is made from red bricks; a blue house is made from blue bricks. So, what is a greenhouse made from?

4. A rancher has 33 heads of cattle standing in a field, when suddenly a bolt of lightning kills all but 9 of them. How many heads of cattle are left standing?

5. John digs a hole that is 2 yards wide, 3 yards long, and 1 yard deep. How many cubic feet of dirt are in it?

6. Two U.S. coins are worth a total of $0.30, and one of them is not a nickel. What are the coins?

7. If a doctor gives you 3 pills and told you to take one every half-hour, how long will it take to finish all 3 pills?

8. If a woman is 21 and is half the age of her mom how old will the mom be when the woman is 42?

9. If you had only one match and you entered a cold, dark room that contained an oil heater, an oil lamp, and a candle, which object would you light first?

10. A man arrives in town on Friday, and he leaves three days later on Saturday. How does he do it?

Fill in each blank with the correct reflexive pronoun in brackets.

1. The peacock is grooming _____ [herself / itself].

2. My aunt is driving _____ [ourselves / herself] to the hospital.

3. My uncles enjoy taking a stroll after dinner by _____ [himself / themselves].

4. Where is the actress working for _____ [herself / itself]?.

5. I want to read the book _____ [ourselves / myself].

6. Don't let the little boy use the knife by _____ [himself / itself]!

7. Take your plate to the sink _____ [themselves / yourself].

8. "Close your eyes and imagine _____ [yourselves / ourselves] in space," the teacher told the children.

9. We can do it _____ [itself / ourselves]. We don't need help.

10. You and your friend should clean up the room _____ [ourselves / yourselves].

Tourism in Korea

Jeonju is the 16th largest city in South Korea and the capital of North Jeolla Province. It is an important tourist center famous for Korean food, historic buildings, and exciting festivals.

In May 2012, Jeonju was chosen as a Creative City for Gastronomy as part of UNESCO's Creative Cities Network. This honor recognizes the city's traditional home cooking handed down from generation to generation over thousands of years. Jeonju is famous for its Korean cuisine and has many well-known and popular restaurants. Jeonju is known as the food capital of Korea and its most loved dish is Jeonju bimbimbap, which is a rice dish with mixed vegetables and red pepper paste.

Many people also visit Jeonju to see and experience traditional Korean houses called "hanok", located in Jeonju's hanok Village. The village is home to many guesthouses re-modeled from old hanok structures, restaurants, cafes, and historical sites. It is one of the top tourist attractions in all of Korea.

vocabulary

- province: 지방, 분야
- cuisine: 요리법, (비싼 식당의) 음식

1. Where is Jeonju located in Korea?

   _____

2. What is Jeonju famous for?

   _____

3. What is the most popular tour site in Jeonju?

   _____

Try to make a short sentence with the word or expression.

1. famous for

   _____

2. hand down

   _____

3. one of the top

   _____

Jeju Island is the largest island off the coast of the Korean Peninsula, and the main island of Jeju Province of South Korea. Jeju Island has the warmest weather in Korea. Even in winter, the temperature rarely falls below 0°C (32°F). Jeju is a popular holiday destination and a center for Korean tourism.

Also known as, "The Hawaii of Korea," many tourists from all over the country and the world visit Jeju Island every year. They enjoy the warm weather and coastal scenery. You can go to the beach and enjoy some fresh local seafood or hike to the peak of Mount Halla. If you are tired of walking, you can go on one of Jeju's famous horseback riding tours!

Jeju Island is also a favorite romantic destination. You can see many couples holding hands on dates at places like the Jeju Teddy Bear Museum or Jeju Loveland.

Whether you are with family, friends or someone special, there is always a lot of fun in the sun on Jeju Island!

---

vocabulary

- horseback: (명사 앞에만 씀)말을 타고 하는
- destination: 목적지, 도착지

1. Where is the center for Korean tourism?

2. What is the name of the highest mountain in Jeju?

3. What is the nickname of Jeju?

Try to make a short sentence with the word or expression.

1. be known as

2. hike

3. whether A or B

Horseback riding

(Robert and Maria talking about recreational activities)

Robert: Hi, Maria. Where are you going?

Maria: I am going to church to meet my friends.

Robert: I see. Are you going anywhere after?

Maria: We have a plan to go to a ranch. We are going horseback riding.

Robert: Is it your first time?

Maria: No, I have tried it twice in Canada. So, this will be my third time.

Robert: Isn't it scary?

Maria: Maybe if it is your first time, but you'll get used to it. How about you, are you doing something fun?

Robert: My father and I will go fishing at the famous lake later.

Maria: I have never tried fishing. I think it's boring. Is it?

Robert: Well, it requires a lot of patience because you might have to wait for a long time. But, you will enjoy once you start.

Maria: Well, have a good time with your father.

Robert: You too!

1. Where is Gary going?

   _____

2. How many times has Gary tried horseback riding?

   _____

3. What is Robert going to do?

   _____

1. I am going to church to meet my friends.
   - My friends and I are going to meet at the church.
   - I will meet my friends at the church.
   - My friends will meet me at church.

2. … but you'll get used to it.
   - …but you'll be accustomed to it.
   - …but you'll adapt to it soon.
   - …but it will become easier to you soon.

3. I think it's boring. Is it?
   - Is it (not) boring?
   - It is boring, isn't it?
   - I think it is uninteresting, isn't it?

Demonstrative Pronouns

Fill in the blanks with this, that, these, or those.

1. _____ is Rover, my pet dog.

2. _____ shop on the next street sells delicious cakes.

3. Take _____. You may need it.

4. _____ clothes on that rack need to be washed. Please put them in the laundry basket.

5. _____ shop is having a big sale. Let's go there!

6. How much are _____ shoes on that shelf?

7. _____ medicine will cure your cold. Take it.

8. I am bringing _____ children to the canteen now.

9. Who has thrown _____ banana peels all over the floor?

10. _____ man has been standing outside our house for an hour!

11. _____ bedroom at the end of the living room is my brother's.

12. Can you see _____ crows perching on _____ tree?

Global Cultures

Korean culture is becoming more and more popular all over the world. The "Korean Wave," also known as, Hallyu, is a global phenomenon that is growing every year. Korea is not only a leader in pop culture, but also famous for traditional culture as well.

Firstly, the entertainment culture of Korea has a strong influence in Asia and even in western countries. An increasing number of people are fans of K-pop, K-dramas, and also the Korean movie industry. For example, K-pop groups like BTS are world-famous and have hundreds of millions of fans globally.

Also, tourism in Korea is expanding. Visitors from all over the world come to enjoy everything an economic and cultural center like Korea can offer, but also to see traditional and historic attractions as well. Korea is a land with a long history and many special customs. There are also a lot of historic sites such as Gyeongbok Palace and Bulguk Temple.

---

vocabulary

- phenomenon: 현상(=happening)
- expand: 확대(확장)하다

1. What is Hallyu?

2. Whom do you know among K-pop idols?

3. What is good to visit in Korea?

Try to make a short sentence with the word or expression.

1. a number of

2. hundreds of millions

3. historic sites

What we know about the American culture is usually referring to culture from the United States. America has a very diverse culture that has influenced the whole world. It is known as the land of the free and opportunity for all. So, it is called a "melting pot."

The United States of America is a huge country with many different regions. Each region has its own unique culture. The East coast is known for cities like New York, Washington, D.C., and Boston. These are some of the oldest cities in the country and they have a rich history and deep culture.

The West coast is known for cities such as Los Angeles and Las Vegas. The western part of America is home to the industries of American entertainment and pop culture. For example, Hollywood movies are seen all over the world and, American pop music is just as popular. Other places such as those in the South or Hawaii, are even more unique and also very interesting.

> **vocabulary**
>
> • diverse: 다양한(=various)
> • huge: 거대한(=enormous, vast)
> • unique: 유일한, 독특한(=unusual)

1. Why is American culture called a "melting pot"?

   _____

2. What can we see on the East coast? How about on the West coast?

   _____

3. Talk about the famous cities of America.

   _____

Try to make a short sentence with the word or expression.

1. be known as

   _____

2. be known for

   _____

3. just as

   _____

K-pop Concert

(George and Emma met at a park one early Monday morning)

George: Hello Frank!

Emma: Good morning, George! Fancy meeting you here.

George: I am just walking my dog. I am heading to the office later. And you?

Emma: I just arrived from Seoul. I went there last weekend.

George: Was it work-related?

Emma: No. I met my boyfriend and we went to see a concert.

George: Whose concert was it?

Emma: Ah. Seoul's Dream Concert. I saw many K-pop groups like EXO, NCT Dream, Twice, Got7, BTS, and other new generation idols.

George: Wow, you must have enjoyed a great concert!

Emma: Yes, I did. It was really fantastic.

George: Were there a lot of people?

Emma: Yes! I even saw many foreigners. That only proves that K-pop is not only loved by Koreans but foreigners as well.

George: Really? Did they sell posters and other merchandise?

Emma: Yes. I was able to buy some photo cards and also some light bands.

1. What are they talking about?

   _____

2. Where did Frank go last weekend?

   _____

3. Describe Frank's experience.

   _____

1. Fancy meeting you here.
   - Good to meet you here.
   - Nice to see you here.
   - I'm glad to see you.

2. Was it work related?
   - Was it related to work?
   - Was it because of work?
   - Did you do work there?

3. K-pop is not only loved by Koreans but foreigners as well.
   - K-pop is loved both by Koreans and foreigners.
   - Both Koreans and foreigners love K-pop.
   - Koreans, as well as foreigners, love K-pop.

Fill in each blank with the correct interrogative pronoun (who, what, whom, which, whose).

1. _____ would you like to have for lunch?

2. _____ of these shops sells towels?

3. With _____ did you walk to school this morning?

4. _____ is your father's name?

5. _____ of these is your bag?

6. _____ are you doing here?

7. _____ wallet is this?

8. To_____ do these umbrellas belong?

9. _____ house do you live in?

10. _____ pencil should I choose?

11. _____ is that man standing beside your car?

12. To _____ are you giving the cake?

Economics

Currency has many names such as cash, capital, or money. Each country has its own currency with its own name and value. We use these currencies to buy goods and services. Also, we can exchange one currency to another currency if we plan to travel or do international business.

South Korean currency is called, "won," and is represented by the symbol, "₩" The Won was created after World War II with the end of Japanese colonial rule. Like all currencies, it is divided into notes and coins. The notes include values from 1,000won to 50,000won, and coins are available from 10won to 500won. They are similar to American bills and coins such as the penny, nickel, dime, quarter, and half dollar coins.

The exchange value of each world currency represents the economic power of the country. Besides the Korean won, other powerful currencies include the US dollar, Japanese yen, Chinese yuian, and the Euro of European Union.

vocabulary

- currency: 통화, 화폐
- represent: 대신하다, 대표하다

1. What is currency?

   _____

2. What are the coins in American currency?

   _____

3. What is an exchange rate in world currency?

   _____

Try to make a short sentence with the word or expression.

1. plan to

   _____

2. be divided into

   _____

3. represent

   _____

There are many huge companies in the world. We call these companies corporations. They have thousands of employees and are very powerful groups. Most of the largest companies have stocks which are publicly traded on the stock market.

Each stock is a small unit of ownership of a company. Corporations sell these stocks to the people for the purpose of raising money. This money or capital is used to expand the business and earn more money. Stocks can be a great investment because they increase in value as the company grows and develops.

Each country has its own stock market. This is where we can buy stocks. In Korea, stocks for companies such as Samsung, LG, Kia, and Hyundai have high value. In America, Google, Apple, and Amazon stocks are popular.

The secret for investing in stocks is to buy low and sell high!

---

vocabulary

- corporation: 기업(회사)
- stock: 주식, 증권

1. What is stock?

_____

2. Why do big companies sell their stocks to people?

_____

3. What can we do with the stocks?

_____

Try to make a short sentence with the word or expression.

1. huge

_____

2. capital

_____

3. popular

_____

Ask and answer your peer's questions and change your role with your partner.

1. Have you ever been another country?

2. How did you get there?

3. Where did you visit and what did you see?

4. Which seat do you want to take in the airplane?

5. Did you buy anything at the duty free?

6. Describe your last summer vacation.

Write a short story about your longest trip. Use the questions as your guide.

Did you go to a very far place? When, where and why did you go?

Whom did you go with? How did you get there?

_____

_____

_____

_____

_____

_____

_____

_____

_____

_____

_____

_____

_____

Unit 10

International

IMF is the abbreviation for the International Monetary Fund. When a nation is in economic difficulties, it helps the country to survive.

The headquarters of the IMF is located in Washington, D.C., USA. It was founded in 1947. It is also called the third currency. This organization unifies the world economy. It has supported the countries which experienced economic crisis. In some cases, people like the IMF because they help third world countries.

On the other hand, people do not like it because it creates too much burden for the countries it helps. In the 1990s, there were many Asian countries which got a loan from the IMF. The economic crisis started in Malaysia.

South Korea was one of the countries it helped. Koreans made many efforts to be free from the difficulties it created. Many people joined the campaign called "Collecting Gold." Eventually, South Korea overcame the economic crisis and today it has one of the most powerful economies in Asia and the world.

---

vocabulary

- abbreviation: 축약형, 약어
- organization: 조직(=group), 단체(=association), 기구
- unify: 통일(통합)하다

1. When was the IMF founded?

2. What does the IMF do for countries?

3. What does IMF mean?

Try to make a short sentence with the word or expression.

1. abbreviation for

2. In some cases

3. free from

WHO is the abbreviation for the World Health Organization. They are interested in the health and well-being of the world. They focus mainly on diseases that could harm entire communities.

The WHO tries to bring fresh water, food, and medicine. They want to stop the spread of diseases throughout the world. They also work for the development of new food resources and medicine. They have helped to stop several kinds of infections such as SARS and the Bird Flu.

The WHO is supporting researchers who can develop new medicine. The Swine Flu is one of their major interests for research. They are trying to find vaccines to prevent the flu and other diseases. The WHO is trying to make this world healthier and free from disease.

vocabulary

- entire: 전체의
- infection: 감염, 전염병
- disease: 질병

1. What does the WHO focus on?

   _____

2. Who does the WHO do for the world?

   _____

3. What do people want from WHO?

   _____

Language Acquisition

Try to make a short sentence with the word or expression.

1. be interested in

   _____

2. focus on

   _____

3. several kinds of

   _____

Language Practice: Q&A Activity and Writing Practice

Volunteering Activities

(Jack and Susan are attending an activity to join a volunteer work at a hospital)

Jack: Hello. My name is Jack. And, you are?

Susan: I'm Susan. Is it your first time to volunteer?

Jack: Hi, Susan. Actually, I have been volunteering for a long time but not at a hospital.

Susan: That's good. This is a new experience for you. This is my first time.

Jack: I see. You know, they say the benefits of volunteering at a hospital are great.

Susan: Oh, really?

Jack: Yes. First, we can meet new people and build new relationships. Our social skills will be improved. Also, we will learn new skills that we cannot learn from our majors or jobs. We can gain experience and improve self-worth.

Susan: You're right. But I also volunteered because for another reason.

Jack: And, what might that be?

Susan: The patients. You know some patients are not visited by anyone. I can be a support to them.

Jack: Oh, yeah. That is also a very good reason. We can help them while they recover from their illnesses.

Susan: Yes. So, I am happy that our university gave us the opportunity to volunteer.

Jack: That's true.

        (The hospital volunteer coordinator enters the hall)

Susan: The coordinator is here. It's time for the meeting.

1. Where are Jack and Susan?

2. What are the benefits of volunteering?

3. Talk about some volunteer work that you know.

1. Our social skills will be improved.
   - Our social skills will be enhanced.
   - We can develop our interpersonal skills.
   - Our interpersonal skills will progress / advance.

2. I also volunteered for another reason.
   - I have another reason for volunteering.
   - My volunteering was due to a different motivation.
   - There is another reason why I volunteered.

3. Some patients are not visited by anyone.
   - Some patients do not have visitors.
   - Nobody visits some patients.
   - There aren't any visitors for some patients.

Simple Present Tense

Fill in each blank with the present tense form of the word in the brackets.

Ali [1] _____ [wake] up at five o'clock every morning. He quickly [2]

_____ [brush] his teeth and [3] _____ [wash] his face before

changing clothes. Then he [4] _____ [eat] a slice of bread with a cup of

hot Milo. After breakfast, he [5] _____ [leave] the house on his bicycle to

deliver newspapers. He [6] _____ [return]to the house at half past six. He [7]

_____ [take] a shower and [8] _____ [get] ready for school. His

neighbor, Choon Seng, always [9] _____ [arrive] punctually at 7 o'clock

at Ali's house. The two school boys then go out and [10] _____ [walk] to

school together.

Modern Technology

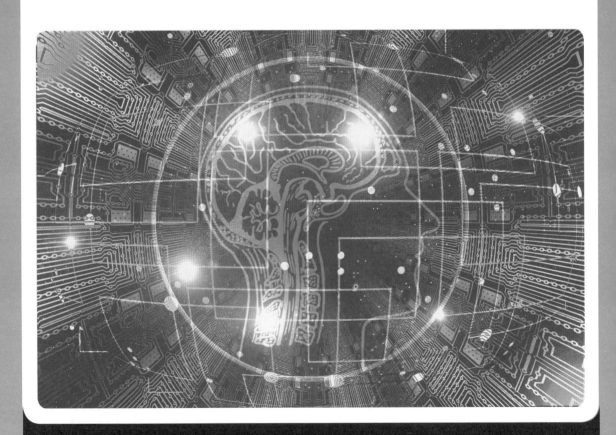

The Electric Car

In busy metropolitan cities like Seoul, there are cars everywhere you look. Cars and other automobiles are a necessity in modern life. They have revolutionized the way we get from place to place.

However, cars also cause problems. They rely on petroleum fuel to power their engines. Oil is a limited resource that is becoming increasingly expensive. Also, this type of energy causes air pollution due to harmful carbon emissions.

Therefore, electric cars have been developed to solve these problems. These days, they are becoming more common and promoted by governments. Major car manufacturing companies are improving their electric car models and the technology is advancing. The electric engines are becoming more powerful and efficient. These engines are clean and electricity is cheap. They use batteries that need to be charged at home or at a charging station. Companies such as Tesla are leading the way for making quality electric cars.

vocabulary

- metropolitan: 대도시의, 수도의
- efficient: 능률적인, 효율적인

1. Why do people need electric cars?

   _____

2. What do we usually need to run a car engine?

   _____

3. What kind of cars do you think will people develop in the future?

   _____

Try to make a short sentence with the word or expression.

1. revolutionized

   _____

2. due to

   _____

3. becoming more

   _____

Have you ever heard of AI? It stands for artificial intelligence. It allows machines to function without human control. These AI controlled computers and machines are programmed to make decisions and take actions using their own intelligence. To put it simply, it is like giving a machine its own brain.

Even today, many human functions are being performed by machines and computers. As AI advances and develops, the need for a human workforce will decrease. Jobs once done by people will be done more efficiently by machines, computer systems, and even robots.

Companies such as Samsung and Google are researching to develop artificial intelligence. Some people are afraid of the problems it might cause, such as job shortages, or even AI becoming too smart and becoming a threat to humankind. On the other hand, the benefits of AI are hard to ignore.

---

vocabulary

- artificial: 인공의, 인조의
- function: 기능
- ignore: 무시하다(=disregard)

1. Does AI have a real brain like human beings?

2. What can AI do instead of people?

3. Is AI a threat to human kind?

Try to make a short sentence with the word or expression.

1. stand for

2. be afraid of

3. artificial

Favorite subject

(Susan and Tom are talking about their subject in the classroom)

Tom: Hello, Susan. How was your midterm exam?

Susan: Hi, Tom. It wasn't too bad.

Tom: I was unlucky with the English test.

Susan: What happened?

Tom: I made a big mistake on the writing part.

Susan: That's too bad. What's your favorite subject, Tom?

Tom: My favorite subject is science and I am interested in AI nowadays.

Susan: Science is not my cup of tea. You mean Artificial Intelligence?

Tom: Yep. It is becoming more interesting to me. We can do a lot of things through AI without human labor.

Susan: But it can take our jobs.

Tom: No, I don't think so. People will find a better way to live with it.

Susan: If you are right, it will be great. I hope you will be a great AI professional someday.

1. What is Tom's favorite subject at school?

   _____

2. What does Tom want to be?

   _____

3. What can we do with AI?

   _____

1. How was your midterm exam?
   - Did you do well on your midterm exam?
   - How did your midterm exam go?
   - Was your midterm exam okay?

2. That's too bad.
   - That's awful.
   - I am sorry to hear that.
   - That's unfortunate.

3. Science is not my cup of tea.
   - I am not interested in science.
   - I do not like science (very much).
   - Science is not my favorite (subject).

Fill in the blanks with the correct verbs in the box.

hide	fetches	chew	wags	run
gave	call	see	play	spend

My uncle [1] _____ me a puppy for my birthday last year.

I [2] _____ him 'Patches' because he has black and brown patches all

over his body.

Patches is an intelligent dog. He [3] _____ the newspaper for my

father every day. However, Patches can be very mischievous too. He likes to [4]

_____ the shoelaces of my shoes and when he sees me coming towards

him, he will run away and [5] _____ from me. When he is happy, he [6]

_____ his tail. Patches is always happy to [7] _____ me come

home from school. Every day, I [8] _____ time with Patches. We [9]

_____ ball in the garden. Sometimes, we [10] _____ in the park

nearby.

Unit 12

The Space Age

Natural Resources in Space

Humans need resources to keep society moving and growing. We depend on resources that come naturally from our planet Earth. The problem is that as more countries become developed and the global population increases, natural resources become less common. As a result, the price increases and competition between countries becomes stronger.

As space age technology develops, one possible solution for this problem could be asteroid mining. Asteroids are large rocks floating in space. There are millions of asteroids just in our own solar system. Many of these rocks are huge and hold a large amount of resources. Valuable minerals such as gold, silver, platinum, and tungsten could be transported back to Earth. Also, minerals such as iron, nickel, aluminum, and titanium can be used to build more structures in space such as space stations, satellites, machinery, and vehicles.

Asteroid mining will be the first step towards building colonies and infrastructure in space. One day, Earth will become too small for humans and we will look to the stars for our future.

---

vocabulary

- resource: 자원, 재원
- asteroid: 소행성
- infrastructure: 사회(공공)기반시설

1. Will we have enough resources on Earth in the near future?

   _____

2. What is asteroid mining?

   _____

3. Why do people want to build space stations?

   _____

Try to make a short sentence with the word or expression

1. depend on

   _____

2. in space

   _____

3. for our future

   _____

Space exploration has been advanced by governments around the world. Space programs such as NASA from the United States and Roscosmos from Russia have led the way for space flight and exploration.

Up to now, only astronauts trained by these government programs have had a chance to fly into space. However, private companies are now able to build space ships that can take common people for space tours!

Companies like SpaceX and Boeing are working with the government to develop commercial space flights. At first, these tours will be very expensive and will only be taken by the very rich, but as time goes on, more and more people will be able to take part. In the future, we will be able to travel in a space tour ship to a space hotel and take a space vacation!

---

vocabulary

- exploration: 탐사, 답사, 탐험
- in the future: 장차, 미래에
- astronaut: 우주비행사(astrology-천문학)

1. Who leads world space programs?

   _____

2. Do you want to go on a space tour in the future?

   _____

3. What is a space vacation?

   _____

Try to make a short sentence with the word or expression

1. Up to now

   _____

2. have a chance to

   _____

3. more and more

   _____

At the lost and found

Brian: Good evening, officer. I just found this briefcase at the subway station.

Officer: Ah. Let's have a look inside. Oh dear! I can't find any ID card. We need the person's name and address.

Brian: Well, there's a laptop computer. I'm sure the owner is looking for it.

Officer: So, you looked inside, didn't you?

Brian: Well, I had a quick look, but I didn't touch anything!

Officer: Here's a name and a number on a business card.

Brian: That's a good clue.

Officer: I will hold on to this until my duty ends. I will hand it over to someone before I go home. Or, I can take it to the police station and post something on our website, hoping for the owner to read it.

Brian: Okay, officer. Thank you. I will be going then.

Officer: Sure. And, good job turning it over. By the way, I need your name and phone number just in case.

Brian: Yes, my name is Brian O'Hara. My number is 555-1125.

Officer: Okay, Brian. I will call you and let you know what happens to this briefcase.

1. Who found a lost briefcase?

_____

2. Where did he find the briefcase?

_____

3. What was in the briefcase?

_____

Substitution Drills

1. Oh dear! (expression of surprise)
   - Oh no!
   - Dear me!
   - Oh my!

2. I will hand it over to someone…
   - I will give it to someone…
   - I will pass it to someone…
   - I will give the responsibility to someone else…

3. By the way,…
   - In addition,…
   - Oh, and one more thing,…
   - Oh, and I need to,…

Fill in each blank with the past continuous form of the verb in the brackets.

1. I _____ [joke]. Please don't take it seriously.

2. Nora _____ [climb] up the ladder to reach the top shelf.

3. You did not see me because you _____ [wash] dishes in the kitchen.

4. "I _____ not _____ [look] at you," he insisted.

5. He _____ [jog] in the park with his friend this morning.

6. Lisa _____ [do] her homework in the room.

7. The boys _____ [eat] first because they were hungry.

8. Linyi and Mei _____ [bake] a cake for their mother.

9. Mr Chia and his family _____ [swim] at Changi Beach last weekend.

10. The pupils _____ [take] an English test yesterday.

11. Siva _____ [feed] his cat a while ago.

12. Little Tim _____ [read] under a tree while the rest of the children

    _____ [play] hide-and-seek.

Unit 13

Electronic Entertainment

Virtual Reality

Electronic entertainment created with computer graphics and animation is always changing and developing. Electronic media such as computer games, started as 2D and evolved into 3D. Nowadays, 3D computer images look almost like the real thing.

The next step is virtual reality. Virtual reality makes the user feel like they are inside the computer-generated world. The users wear headsets that create 3D images that surround them in every direction. The users feel as if they are in the middle of a 3D environment that they can move around in and interact with.

This creates a new level of immersion. Instead of staring at a screen and using a game pad, players will walk around, run, jump, and use gestures to perform actions in the game. One problem is that virtual worlds might become so fun to play in, people might like it better than the real world!

vocabulary

• virtual reality: 가상현실
• immersion: 통합, 결합

1. What was the first type of computer games?

_____

2. What do you think VR is?

_____

3. Why do people like to play with VR?

_____

Try to make a short sentence with the word or expression

1. in the middle of

_____

2. instead of

_____

3. better than

_____

Traditional sports are loved by many people. They are a great way to spend time and have some exercises. They require physical strength and athletic ability. They are a great way to experience and enjoy competition. But, nowadays, many people enjoy the competition of Electronic Sports or E-Sports.

E-Sports don't depend on physical attributes, but rely on the players' skills in computer games. Teams or individuals compete against each other by playing popular games in a league or tournament. Millions of fans watch these games online or live in person. They cheer for their favorite teams or pro-gamers, just like they do for other sports.

E-Sports is a big industry where the best pros get paid a lot of money and team owners have sponsorships and advertising deals with major companies. E-sports is very popular in Korea. For example, games such as Overwatch and League of Legends have exciting pro leagues with many fans. Many young children dream of becoming a pro-gamer one day.

---

vocabulary

- compete against: ~과 경쟁하다. 서로 대치하다
- sponsorship: 후원, 지원

1. What are the differences between traditional sports and E-Sports?

2. Why do a lot of people enjoy E-Sports?

3. What is a pro-gamer?

Try to make a short sentence with the word or expression.

1. rely on

2. deal with

3. dream to become

Sports

Sports are an important and healthy part of all students' lives. Of course, sports can be important in everyone's life, but sports are especially important to students. This is because sports can affect students in ways that will help them for the rest of their lives. Parents and school should encourage children to play sports for all of the benefits that sports provide. There are a lot of reasons why sports can benefit a student.

First, sports are good for students because it is an excellent exercise. To have good health, it is necessary for students to exercise often. Playing sports such as soccer, basketball, or baseball are excellent ways for students to be healthy. These days students must study very hard to succeed in life. Regular exercise will help them have a healthy body and healthy mind.

Second, sports help students learn about working together. Team sports require students to cooperate. Learning cooperation is a very important skill for their lives. In a company, just like a sports team, people must work together. We must learn to help each other to achieve a goal. Playing sports can help students be ready for the future.

To conclude, sports are good for students for many reasons. Some of the most important reasons are that sports make students healthier, and also teach them how to cooperate better for a goal. Being healthy and having good cooperating skills are two very important things for students to learn and to keep for the rest of their lives. Since students can gain both of these qualities from sports, they benefit students in very positive ways.

Write an essay according to the given statement.

Statement: Sports are beneficial to young students.

Fill in each blank with the correct preposition in the box.
Use each word once only.

to	behind	in	through	at	on
out	up	between	above	from	into

The children are [1] _____ school. They climb [2] _____ the stairs to go [3] _____ their classrooms.

They are sitting [4] _____ their desks. Joel sits [5] _____ Wei Lun and Timothy. His best friend, Sean, sits [6] _____ Rachel because he is taller.

The children place their schoolbags [7] _____ the floor. They take out their books and pencils [8] _____ their bags.

Suddenly, a sparrow flies [9] _____ their classroom. It flies [10] _____ their heads and finally out [11] _____ the window. The teacher then gives [12] _____ the worksheets and continues the lesson.

Unit 14

English Immersion

The education system in Korea can be quite stressful. The competition to get into a good university affects even young children in elementary school. So, many Korean students dream of studying abroad in English- speaking countries such as the United States or Canada.

In America, school life isn't as difficult as in Korea. Students have more time to enjoy the beautiful surroundings and more chances to relieve stress. Students can attend elementary to high school in the public school system or attend a private institute to focus on special skills.

Some older Korean students attend universities in America. There, they can get a bachelor's, master's, or doctorate degrees. A degree from a university in America is great for getting a job in both America and Korea and also in other countries. Other students attend summer or winter camps in America or some other English-speaking countries and have a lot of wonderful experiences.

---

vocabulary

- focus on: ~집중해서, ~에 초점을 맞추어
- doctorate: 박사의, 박사

1. Why do you think students in Korea want to study abroad?

   _____

2. What is English immersion?

   _____

3. What do students to develop their English?

   _____

Try to make a short sentence with the word or expression.

1. dream of

   _____

2. stressful

   _____

3. as difficult as

   _____

International Schools

English immersion is the best and fastest way to study the language. Immersion means that you live your life in a place where a foreign or second language is spoken. Full English immersion means you study all your classes in English and live your home and personal life in English as well. This can be done by studying abroad and staying in a home with a local family in that area.

However, in Korea, students can attend an English immersion school to master English. These schools are often called International Schools. All the teachers at an International School are usually qualified teachers from native English-speaking countries. They teach all subjects in English just like in America. In fact, many of these schools are certified by the American school system. That means it is the same as attending an American school.

International schools are a great way to improve your English to a very high level. Not only can you improve your English, but it is also a great way to be accepted at an American university.

---

vocabulary

- qualified: 자격을 갖춘, 유자격의
- certified: 인증된 인증되어진

1. Where can we get an English immersion education?

   _____

2. What is an International school?

   _____

3. What can we achieve from the international school?

   _____

Language Acquisition

Try to make a short sentence with the word or expression.

1. the best way to

   _____

2. as well

   _____

3. Not only + but also

   _____

Sample essay

Fast food

Fast food is becoming a major problem in today's society. It is easy to see that fast food is becoming more and more popular all the time. With so many fast food restaurants being built, it is easier for people to buy fast food instead of cooking meals at home. This is causing many different problems in our world.

To begin with, fast food which includes pizza and hamburgers contains fats that have been shown to cause high cholesterol levels in many people. High cholesterol can be a major health risk and can lead to such health problems as stroke and heart attacks. Furthermore, it is obvious that fast food causes many people to be overweight. Carrying too much extra fat is known to be harmful to one's health.

The second negative effect of fast food is that it shortens the amount of time families spend together. Dining together as a family creates much needed social time for a family. It allows a family to interact with each other.

However, fast food meals are replacing regular family time. Therefore, fast food makes relationship among family members weaker than regular meals do.

In conclusion, the amount of fast food in our society is leading to many harmful effects to people. The negative effects of fast food impact two important areas in a person's life. These areas are health and social relationships. It is harmful to our health because of the amount of grease and fat contained in fast food. Also, it is harmful to social relationships because it decreases the amount of time a family spends together. The negative impacts of fast food on these two important areas of life prove that fast food is a serious problem in modern society.

Answer the questions below about the essay above.

1. What's the topic sentence of the essay?

   _____

2. What are the supporting ideas of the essay?
   a.

   _____

   b.

   _____

3. What is the concluding sentence?

   _____

Now, think of the topic sentence, supporting ideas, and concluding sentence of your own essay regarding the topic, "Eat Healthy to a Better You."

1. Topic sentence

   _____

2. Supporting sentences (2-3)

   _____

   _____

   _____

3. Concluding sentence

   _____

Prepositions of Time

Fill in each blank with the correct preposition.

1. We must hand in our homework _____ Monday.

2. I am going to church _____ Sundays.

3. We are going out at 5 PM. Can you finish your homework _____ then?

4. Will you go to New Zealand _____ 5th June?

5. My family will go on a vacation _____ December.

6. Will you come home in time _____ lunch?

7. You can go out to play only _____ you have completed your work.

8. We waited _____ Mother to return from work to ask for her permission to go out.

9. May bids her parents good night _____ she goes to bed.

10. I can't wait _____ the holidays to come. Me parents are taking me to Disneyland.

11. We must complete the test _____ 12 noon today.

Unit 15

Globalization

Multinational Companies

In the modern era, the largest companies in the world have much power. These corporations in Korea such as Samsung, Hyundai, LG, and Kia control much of the economy. Giant companies in America like Google, Amazon, Microsoft, and Apple are the same.

These huge companies not only do business at home but also, they have a lot of international businesses. They have headquarters, offices, and production plants all over the world. The have marketing teams that focus on different regions. For example, Hyundai sells many cars in America. They have an American headquarters and thousands of American employees. They marke cars to American people. Sometimes, the names of the cars are even different.

Language skills are very important in these multinational companies. There must be constant communication between the home country and international branches. These companies hire many people with interpretation and translation skills.

vocabulary

- headquarter: 본사, 에 본부를 두다
- multinational: 다국적의
- interpretation: 해석, 이해, 설명(=explanation)

1. What is a multinational company?

   _____

2. Name some multinational companies that you know.

   _____

3. What do you think you need to get a job at a multinational company?

   _____

Try to make a short sentence with the word or expression

1. all over the world

   _____

2. constant communication

   _____

3. interpretation and translation skills

   _____

Multinational Companies sell their products and services all over the globe. They try to make products with universal appeal that anyone would like. However, cultures are very different and so are regional preferences.

International marketing teams consider regional differences and preferences and create new or redesigned products for each international market. They consider the culture, language, and target market. For example, McDonald's has offices in almost every country in the world. They create different menus for each country. In Korea, the Bulgogi Burger is very popular, but it is not on the American menu.

People who want to be international marketers should understand their target market. People who market for the American region should have lived in America for a long time. Also, they should have fluent English language skills. Samsung is a Korean company that sells a lot of products, such as smart phones and televisions in America. They have a huge international marketing team that focuses on that region.

---

vocabulary

- product: 상품, 물품(=goods)
- regional: 지역의, 지방의
- redesign: 다시 디자인하다

1. Are you familiar with any different cultures?

2. What do we need to be a global marker?

3. Do the multinational companies have the same products for all over the world?

Try to make a short sentence with the word or expression.

1. fluent

2. regional preferences

3. target market

Thanksgiving

Thanksgiving is an important holiday in America and Canada. It is held on the second Monday in October, in Canada, and on the fourth Thursday in November in the U.S. Many Americans and Canadians celebrate Thanksgiving every autumn because they are grateful to have plenty of good food to eat and comfortable lives.

The custom began several hundred years ago when the first pilgrims settled in the New World. At that time, the country was new to the people who came from Europe. They learned how to grow vegetables like corn and squash from the native people who had been living in the country for thousands of years. They also learned to hunt wild turkeys and pick cranberries. This helped them to survive the cold winters for the first few years.

Nowadays, Americans and Canadians get together for a big Thanksgiving dinner. They eat roasted turkey with stuffing, cranberry sauce, potatoes, and other vegetables. For dessert there is usually pumpkin pie. Everyone always enjoys Thanksgiving dinner.

1. When is Thanksgiving?

2. Why do Americans and Canadians celebrate Thanksgiving?

3. What kind of meat do people eat for Thanksgiving dinner?

1. They learned how to grow vegetables.
   - They learned how to cultivate vegetables.
   - They were taught how to grow vegetables.
   - They understood how to grow vegetables.

2. This helped them to survive the cold winters.
   - They survived the cold winters because of this.
   - This assisted them in surviving the cold winters.
   - This helped them (to) endure the cold winters.

3. They eat roasted turkey with stuffing.
   - Roasted turkey with stuffing is eaten.
   - They eat stuffed, roasted turkey.
   - Stuffed roasted turkey is eaten.

Fill in each blank with a suitable preposition.

1. We wake up _____ 8 am sharp every day.

2. She placed the plate in the space _____ the fork and the knife.

3. Please put the books back _____ the shelves.

4. You can watch television _____ you finish your dinner.

5. My grandfather will go swimming with me _____ Sunday.

6. Jane is taller than I. she sits _____ me in class.

7. Where did you come _____?

8. He is climbing _____ the ladder to repair the lamp.

9. The baby boy is crawling _____ his mother.

10. I enjoy traveling _____ the dark tunnel.

11. Timmy is sitting _____ the fan because he feels hot.